FILM

Published by Smart Apple Media
123 South Broad Street
Mankato, Minnesota 56001

Copyright © 2000 Smart Apple Media.
International copyrights reserved in all countries. No
part of this book may be reproduced in any form
without written permission from the publisher.
Printed in the United States of America.

Photos: page 7, 10–CORBIS/Bettmann;
page 13–CORBIS; page 15–CORBIS/Paul Scheult: Eye
Ubiquitous; page 17–CORBIS/Hulton-Deutsch Collec-
tion; page 18–CORBIS; page 19–CORBIS/Bettmann;
page 25–CORBIS/Kurt Krieger; page 27–CORBIS/
Catherine Karnow; page 28–CORBIS/Jim Sugar Photography; page 30–CORBIS/Bettmann

Design and Production: EvansDay Design

Library of Congress Cataloging-in-Publication Data
Vander Hook, Sue, 1949–
Film / by Sue Vander Hook
p. cm. – (Making contact)
Includes index.
Summary: Examines the origins and art of filmmak-
ing from its earliest days to the digitized, computer-
ized films of today.
ISBN 1-887068-65-1
1. Cinematography—History—Juvenile literature.
2. Motion pictures—Production and direction—
Juvenile literature. [1. Cinematography. 2. Motion
pictures—Production and direction.] I. Title.
II. Series: Making contact (Mankato, Minn.)

TR848.V36   1999
791.43'09—dc21   98-35273

First edition

9 8 7 6 5 4 3 2 1

FILM

MAKING CONTACT

SUE VANDER HOOK

"LET'S GO TO A MOVIE!" IT HAS become one of today's most common expressions. Millions of people flock to movie theaters every week. Hundreds of thousands more rent videos every day. What is it that is so attractive about the movies? People are drawn by a number of things: amazing special effects, the **illusion** of another on-screen world, a temporary escape from reality. But movies didn't start out as any of these things. They began more than 100 years ago as a desire to simply capture and recreate the reality of motion.

The human body's visual system has a built-in form of entertainment. If you have ever looked out the window of a moving car, you have watched an amazing motion picture. Your eyes were capturing a kind of "movie" as millions of images, one right after the other, passed by. Motion pictures were born when people began seeking ways to permanently capture such **optical** entertainment.

The desire to preserve what we see began with photography, but people were being entertained by pictures even before that. In the mid-1700s, families would gather to watch shadows on a wall. This early entertainment, called the Magic Lantern, was produced by first painting an image on a piece of glass, then using a bright light and a magnifying lens to project shadows of the image onto a wall.

An artist named Robert Barker later surrounded audiences with a gigantic painting **illuminated** by many different kinds of light. His Panorama, as it was called, quickly spread throughout Europe. Dioramas, in which a large rotating theater moved audiences from one lit painting to another, were also popular at the time.

Another artist came very close to achieving a critical part of the cinema as we know it today. Like modern animation filmmakers, Emile Reynaud drew pictures—called *Pantomimes Lumineuses*—**frame** by frame on a continuous **transparent** strip. A light reflected the drawings off of spinning mirrors, passed them through a lens, and projected them onto a screen. Reynaud's technique created the illusion of movement, but it was jerky and slow, more like a **flip book** than a cartoon. Nonetheless, the modern cinema was one step closer to realization.

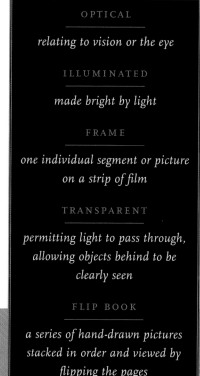

OPTICAL
———
relating to vision or the eye

ILLUMINATED
———
made bright by light

FRAME
———
one individual segment or picture on a strip of film

TRANSPARENT
———
permitting light to pass through, allowing objects behind to be clearly seen

FLIP BOOK
———
a series of hand-drawn pictures stacked in order and viewed by flipping the pages

7

✳ A SPINNING IMAGE PROJECTOR CREATED BY MOTION-PICTURE PIONEER EMILE REYNAUD.

Photographers during the mid-19th century were also searching for ways to make images appear to move. At first, they took pictures of people in several **successive** poses; the person doing the posing would move just enough so each picture looked like the next part of an action. This process took a long time and was tiring for the model. A better method was discovered not by photographers, but by scientists trying to analyze movement.

Eadweard Muybridge, a scientist and professional English photographer, came to the United States in the 1850s. One day he was asked by Governor Stanford of California to take some photographs of the governor's favorite racehorse in action. Muybridge placed a series of cameras alongside the race track. As the governor's horse ran by, it touched a series of cords, triggering the cameras along the way. The governor got photographs of his horse, and Muybridge was able to study motion. His series of pictures in **sequence** created the illusion of motion, laying the foundation for motion pictures.

Several decades later, another scientist named Etienne Marey was drawing pictures of the mechanics of birds in flight. To improve the

Thomas Edison at first forgot to get a patent on his Kinetoscope, and people all over the world were copying his idea and making their own peepshows. To protect his invention, Edison refused to supply these people with the film they needed.

SUCCESSIVE

one right after the other

SEQUENCE

*the following of one thing
after another*

9

✳ EADWEARD MUYBRIDGE'S FAMOUS PHOTOGRAPHS OF A RUNNING RACEHORSE.

accuracy of his drawings, he made a device that could take 12 quick photos of a flying bird, all in one second. In 1888, Marey developed a camera that could take numerous photographs on a continuous strip of **film**.

When the famous inventor Thomas Edison met Muybridge and Marey, he came up with the idea for a motion picture camera. George Eastman, the inventor of the Kodak camera, provided Edison with roll film that was 1 3/8 inches (35 mm) wide. This film, which moved smoothly from one frame to the next, would eventually become the standard size for motion pictures. By 1894, W. K. L. Dickson, the head of Edison's laboratory, had successfully created the Kinetograph, a camera with a mo-

The Kinetoscope was basically a box with a loop of film inside. As a person peered through a tiny hole and the lens, film sped past the viewer's eye at about 48 frames per second.

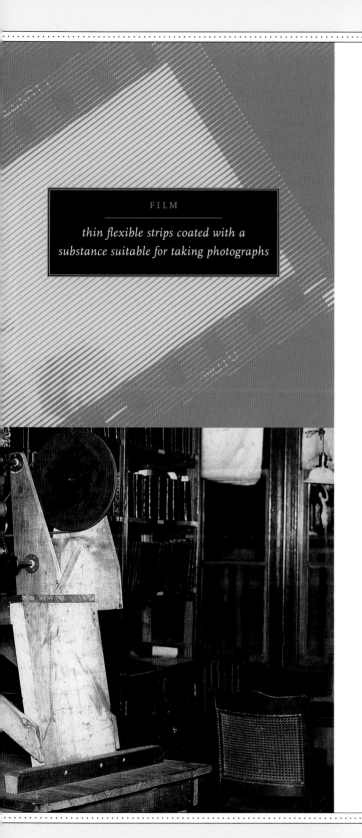

FILM
───────────
*thin flexible strips coated with a
substance suitable for taking photographs*

tor that allowed it to take up to 40 pictures per second.

Edison soon built a motion picture studio on his laboratory property. His studio, called the Black Maria, was just a tar paper hut with a roof that opened to let in the sun. At one end stood the heavy Kinetograph camera; at the other end were various actors and performers. Action films shot at the Black Maria were viewed in a hand-held device called a Kinetoscope. Penny arcades, which were similar to today's video arcades, let audiences look into the Kinetoscope for the price of a penny. These peepshows, as they were called, entertained people with films that lasted no more than 40 to 50 seconds. People marveled at motion pictures of workers demolishing walls and ocean waves breaking on the shore.

✳ THOMAS EDISON AND HIS LATE 19TH-CENTURY MOTION PICTURE CAMERA.

The race soon began to project motion pictures onto a large screen. In France in 1895, the Lumière brothers created the Cinématographe, the first projection device. The next year in the United States, Edison **patented** a projector called the Vitascope. His projector contained a roll of film with a continuous row of holes on each side. A claw-like device in the projector grabbed the film at these holes and pulled it down into the film gate. A beam of light illuminated the frames as they passed by, projecting the series of pictures onto a screen. These pictures jumped and flickered as frames passed slowly by.

The first special effect was created by accident in the 1890s. Georges Méliès was filming traffic on a Paris street. As a bus passed by, his camera jammed. As the camera started working again, a hearse passed by. On the developed film, the bus appeared to suddenly turn into a hearse.

EDISON'S GREATEST MARVEL

THE VITASCOPE

"Wonderful is The Vitascope. Pictures life size and full of color. Makes a thrilling show."
NEW YORK HERALD, April 24, '96.

PATENT
_____
an official government document giving an inventor the exclusive right to make, use, and sell an invention for a certain number of years

13

✳ NEAR THE TURN OF THE CENTURY, FILM AUDIENCES MARVELED AT THE NEWLY DEVELOPED VITASCOPE.

From Silence to Sound

The earliest films were silent ones that lasted less than a minute. Their titles told what they were about: *Arrival of a Train* or *Workers Leaving a Factory*. Soon, penny arcades were turned into five-cent movie theaters called Nickelodeons. With California's year-round sunshine providing great light

for filming, Hollywood soon became the center of American film production. Studios, called "factories," were making one or two films a week, and a reel was now 5 to 10 minutes long.

The Great Train Robbery of 1903 was among the first films produced using new editing techniques. Edwin S. Porter, the film's director, filmed scenes in more than one place, then cut, or **edited**, the film. When he pieced the film together again, it presented action in more than one setting. Films no longer had to be lengthy shots of continuous events in real time; scenes could shift from place to place as multiple stories were developed.

Porter also used some of the most advanced special effects of the time. Large, realistic paintings were used as a background while live action was filmed in front of them. This **matte** technique made it look like scenes had been filmed in exotic, far-off places. Much later,

In the 1950s, when movie makers were trying to woo audiences to the theaters, producers tried using Smell-O-Vision. The process sent out odors that matched the scene on the screen.

EDIT

to prepare and arrange for production

MATTE

a dull finished surface that does not reflect light well

COMPOSITED

made by combining things or parts

mattes were filmed by covering up part of the camera lens to create blank spots on the film. After the film was shot and rewound, the part already filmed was covered up, and live action or special effects were filmed on the blank spots. As matte shots became more sophisticated, two scenes—one of the matte and one of live action—were filmed separately. These two films were then **composited**, or put together, into one scene.

Filmmakers also found ways to create various illusions. Sometimes actors or **miniature** models were suspended on wires and filmed in front of a black or white screen. A background of moving scenery was filmed separately, then the two films were composited together to create the illusion of flight. This technique was the basis for the modern bluescreen method of filming one scene

15

* MINIATURE SETS SUCH AS THIS CITY ALLOW FILMMAKERS TO CREATE STUNNING VISUAL EFFECTS.

in front of a background that can be edited out and replaced with another.

Illusions were also created using miniature sets. Accurate, detailed landscapes and cities were built on a small scale. A camera placed between this miniature set and a full-size one was aimed toward the small set. A sheet of glass—with a specially-shaped mirror where the actor would appear—was then placed in front of the camera lens. As the camera filmed the miniature set, the actor was reflected in the small mirrored area, creating the illusion of matching size. This technique allowed filmmakers to bring exotic locations such as the Greek Parthenon or first-century Rome into American studios of the 1920s.

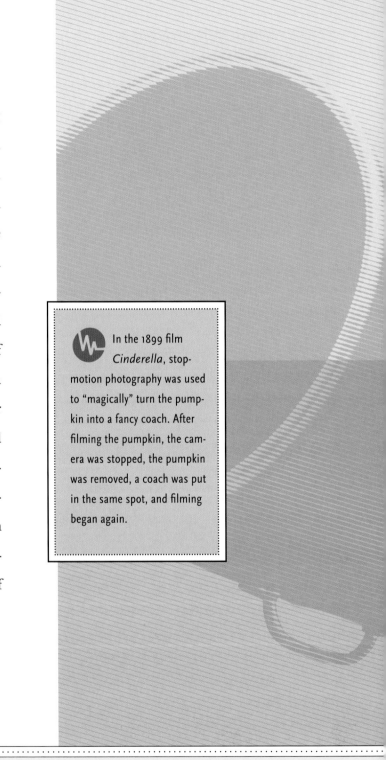

In the 1899 film *Cinderella*, stop-motion photography was used to "magically" turn the pumpkin into a fancy coach. After filming the pumpkin, the camera was stopped, the pumpkin was removed, a coach was put in the same spot, and filming began again.

D. W. Griffith, the director of several early historic films, introduced many of cinema's most important editing techniques: the close-up, the panoramic long shot, the fade-in and fade-out, and crosscutting, which was used to imply action in more than place. Editing techniques and special effects slowly advanced, but sound was still missing.

Many silent films had accompanying music that was played live on a piano in theaters. When sound was actually recorded for a particular film, the actors had to time their actions to match the sound, which was not easy to do. In the 1920s, the Western Electric Company was working on putting sound and pictures on the

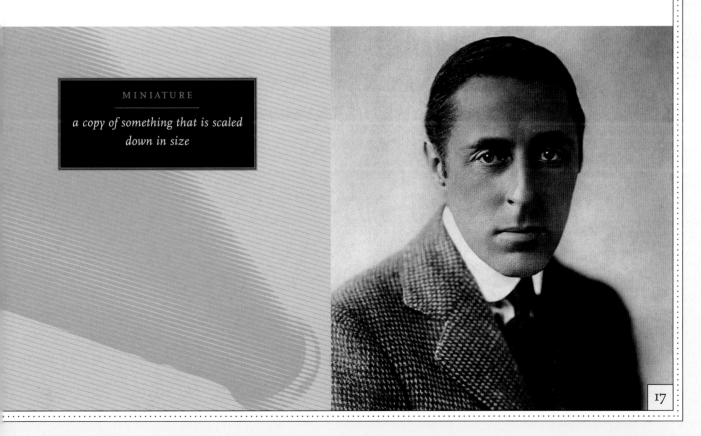

MINIATURE

a copy of something that is scaled down in size

17

same film. After all other studios shied away from its expensive process, Western Electric convinced the struggling Warner Brothers studio to try it.

At first, sound systems used a record that was started at the same time as the film, but pictures and sound were usually **unsynchronized**. Soon, record players were mechanically linked to the projector to coordinate the sound and the action on-screen. This record system turned out to be a disaster, however; when records broke or jumped, everything was thrown out of **sync**. In 1927, Warner Brothers filmed *The Jazz Singer*, the first "talkie," or movie in which someone spoke. Record sound sys-

18

* BY 1910, THEATERS SUCH AS THIS ONE IN ST. LOUIS WERE MAJOR ENTERTAINMENT SOURCES.

tems were soon replaced by sound recorded along the side of the film. Greatly improved through the years, this type of optical sound track is still in use today.

Although sound expanded film's capabilities, it also presented new limitations for directors. The new sound-based camera had to run at 24 frames per second, the speed necessary for sound reproduction. Old special effects techniques created by altering the speed at which film was cranked through the camera were no longer possible. But despite some of the obstacles it presented, sound was definitely a success; by 1929, three-fourths of all films made in Hollywood had sound.

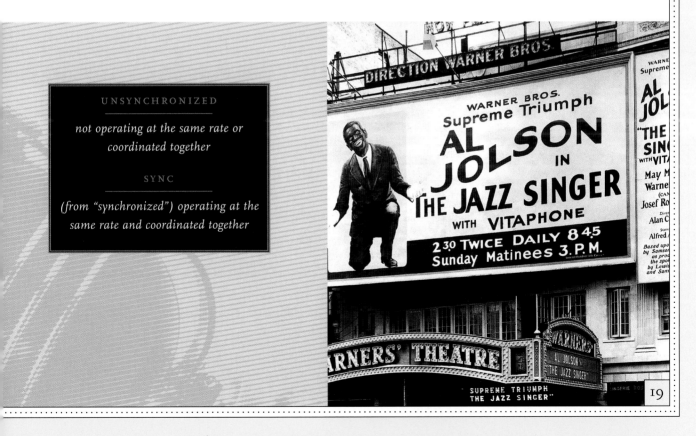

UNSYNCHRONIZED

not operating at the same rate or coordinated together

SYNC

(from "synchronized") operating at the same rate and coordinated together

19

* A 1927 ADVERTISEMENT FOR *THE JAZZ SINGER*, THE FIRST MOVIE WITH SPOKEN WORDS.

With the 1930s came movies in bright, living color. Earlier films were hand-painted or colored by some other method. Films produced in realistic colors became possible with the introduction of three-color Technicolor. Color cameras held three rolls of film that were photographed at the same time to record three separate images of the scene—one in red, one in green, and one in blue. These three images were then combined into one full-color print. For 17 years, all color films used this Technicolor system.

Although audiences were awed by the new color and sound, television nearly destroyed the cinema. Many people preferred to be entertained at home, and the number of moviegoers decreased from about 90 million people in 1948 to only 60 million in 1950. As thousands of cinemas closed down, Hollywood fought back with several technical advances.

In 1933, *Time* magazine reported that King Kong—the "Eighth Wonder of the World"—was 50 feet (15.2 m) tall and 36 feet (11 m) around the chest. In reality, the ape was a miniature model only 18 inches (45.7 cm) tall.

The Eastman Kodak Company produced a single-strip color film. Movies in 3-D (three-dimensions) were made for use with special glasses that merged split images to create depth. Stereo sound was produced by recording on two to seven tracks at a time. Speakers were placed across the front, the sides, and the

21

* THE TECHNICOLOR CAMERA USHERED IN A NEW ERA OF BRIGHT, FULL-COLOR MOVIES.

rear of theaters to create a huge sound field known in the industry as "the surrounds," and later as "surround sound." New magnetic sound tracks could be put only onto wider films measuring 70mm, an expense that made premium sound available only in the biggest cinemas.

Just in time to save the struggling movie industry, the Cinerama came along in 1952. This amazing system, filmed in 70mm, used three cameras and projectors all running at once to beam images simultaneously onto a huge, curved screen. This technique attempted to duplicate the eye's **peripheral** vision and create an image realistic enough to trick the mind. Cinerama reached its peak in 1968 with *2001:*

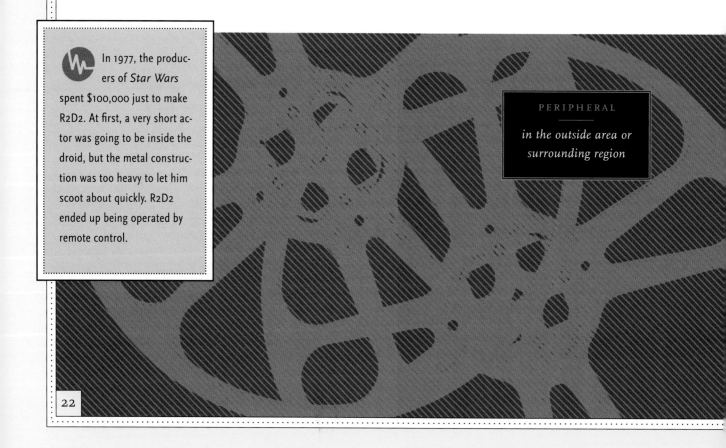

In 1977, the producers of *Star Wars* spent $100,000 just to make R2D2. At first, a very short actor was going to be inside the droid, but the metal construction was too heavy to let him scoot about quickly. R2D2 ended up being operated by remote control.

PERIPHERAL

in the outside area or surrounding region

A Space Odyssey, a film that successfully captured the enormity of outer space.

Cinerama's popularity compelled movie studios to come up with new systems of their own. CinemaScope, VistaVision, Todd-AO, and Panavision were just a few systems that created a bigger and better wide-screen, stereo experience. Soon, only one projector and one wide strip of color 70mm film were needed to change the normal square screen projection into a wide, curved projection. Some studios used a lens that squeezed a wide image into a standard frame of film; the image was unsqueezed by a special lens on the projector. Another technique turned the strip of film 45 degrees while photographing, then projected the film horizontally, stretching it to fit the screen.

✱ SOPHISTICATED CAMERAS AND SKILLED CAMERA CREWS MAKE TODAY'S FILM IMAGES CLEARER THAN EVER.

The mind-blowing special effects of many of today's blockbuster movies actually have roots nearly 100 years old. Viewers of Edison's Kinetoscope watched the Queen of Scotland get beheaded, not knowing that a dummy was substituted for the live actress. The tornado in *The Wizard of Oz* that lifted Dorothy out of Kansas was nothing more than a woman's stocking with air blowing through it.

The great white shark in *Jaws* was actually three different mechanical sharks: Bruce I, Bruce II, and Bruce III, each named after the director's lawyer. One was used for filming shots of the mouth and head; the others were used for side shots.

Through the 1960s, movie makers made little progress in special effects technology. In fact, except for *2001: A Space Odyssey*, the further development of special effects had been ignored almost completely. It wasn't until the mid-1970s that effects again became an important part of movies. At the forefront of this new industry was a young man named George Lucas. To create realistic space settings and effects for his film *Star Wars*, Lucas established a special effects company called Industrial Light and Magic (ILM) and hired John Dykstra of Cinerama to head it up.

In order to create a different kind of space travel from what had been seen before, Dykstra redesigned a basic, computer-controlled camera that previously had been used only for television commercials. The result was the DykstraFlex camera. This sophisticated motion-control camera used computers to recreate camera movement from shot to shot. For the first time, effects technicians could overlap shots of moving scenes, a technique used to create the illusion of warfare in deep space. Later, an optical printer called "The Quad" was developed that allowed the camera to record two separate images simultaneously.

Star Wars was the first feature film to use Dykstra's computer-driven camera. During production of *The Empire Strikes Back*, the sequel to *Star Wars*, ILM developed Go-

25

✳ EFFECTS CREATOR RAY HARRYHAUSEN AND HIS FAMOUS *KING KONG* MOVIE MODEL.

Motion, a technique that animated a miniature creature so it could actually move in front of a rolling camera, eliminating time-consuming frame-by-frame animation. The art of matte painting was taken to new heights in many space scenes in which live-action shots of actors were later inserted over scenery filmed earlier.

In the 1980s, **morphing** was introduced, allowing one image to be progressively altered to transform into another image. In *The Abyss* in 1989, director James Cameron created a water creature entirely by computer. The creature, which could change form from one second to the next, was then mixed with live-action shots using Photoshop, a software program designed to manipulate pictures.

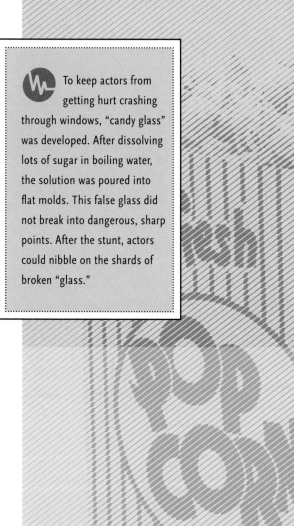

To keep actors from getting hurt crashing through windows, "candy glass" was developed. After dissolving lots of sugar in boiling water, the solution was poured into flat molds. This false glass did not break into dangerous, sharp points. After the stunt, actors could nibble on the shards of broken "glass."

MORPH

(from "metamorphose") to undergo
a complete change in appearance

27

✳ MANY OF TODAY'S MOST POPULAR FILMS ARE FOUNDED ON BRILLIANT SPECIAL EFFECTS.

A composer usually writes the music for a movie at the end of production. The music is recorded, mixed with the dialogue and sound effects, and finally synchronized with the film. The sound track is photographed to create an optical sound track and put on a magnetic strip.

By 1991, ILM and Kodak had created a system that changed each frame of film into many small squares of **digital** information. Each frame, which consisted of 20 **megabytes** of digital information, could be manipulated in any way imaginable. A year after this development, famous filmmaker Steven Spielberg was busy filming *Jurassic Park*. He had been filming dinosaur action by shooting a few frames, moving the huge dinosaur models several inches, and then shooting another few frames. When he learned about the new digital effects, Spielberg immediately dropped this time-consuming

✳ DIGITAL EDITING MACHINES ALLOW FILMMAKERS TO CREATE BELIEVABLE MOTION BY COMPUTER.

stop-action animation and changed to computer-generated special effects. The result was the most realistic, believable dinosaurs ever seen on the big screen. Digital technology was also used in the 1994 production of *Forrest Gump*. Old film of the late president John F. Kennedy was combined with new film of Forrest and manipulated on a computer, allowing Forrest to interact with Kennedy 31 years after the president's death.

In preparation for the 20th anniversary of *Star Wars*, experts began restoring the movie's original film in 1995. The film was cleaned, and computer-generated effects were added. For example, a scene of a newly computerized Jabba the Hutt was added to film previously cut from the original

DIGITAL

a coding system based on numbers; used by computers to read information

MEGABYTE

a term that indicates a standard amount of information storage space on a computer (about 1,000,000 bytes)

When making hand-drawn cartoons and animated films, a camera is suspended above the horizontal table on which the figure has been drawn and placed over a background. Figures are photographed one after the other, creating the illusion of movement. This old-style animation continues to be used today.

Star Wars. With computers, new effects and improvements can now be added to films produced decades ago.

As the booming movie industry begins its second century, studios continue to seek ways to revolutionize filmmaking. For many years to come, film technology will continue to grow and change, perhaps bringing better computer manipulation or making the film industry totally digital. But whatever changes come, the thrill that moviegoers have known since the days of the penny arcade promises to live on.

✳ A SCENE FROM *KING KONG*, A PREMIER EXAMPLE OF EARLY CINEMA'S GREATEST THRILLS.

✳ MODERN COMPUTERS CONTINUE TO MAKE THE IMPOSSIBLE POSSIBLE ON THE BIG SCREEN.